Th...

of Exam Skills

Kate Brookes

Hodder
Children's
Books

Hodder Children's Books
a division of Hodder Headline Limited
338 Euston Road
London NW1 3BH

Printed and bound in France by Brodard & Taupin

'Every moment we are shaping the history of the next.' Paul Brunton, 'What is Karma?'

Exam revision and exams are no one's idea of a fun way to fill a window in your diary, but this Little Book is brimming with the hottest techniques and nifty tricks that will make revision easier. It shows you how important it is to take regular breaks and to relax, how to make your memory more efficient, and how to maximise your exam results. The first part of the book is devoted to revision and memory techniques, with exam skills following on.

DEFINITION

What is revising?

Revising is going over what
you've studied or learned
until you know it, understand
it and can recall it.

NOTE IT

How is revision done?

Different methods work for different people. However, the most common method is condensing all of your work into a more manageable size by writing revision notes.

MOUNTAINS
INTO
MOLEHILLS

*Terrified by the sheer bulk of what
you have to do?*

Turn that mountain of revision into
tiny molehills by breaking each subject
into topics, and each topic into even
smaller units. Write a list of all revision
units and plan these into your
revision timetable.

TAKE THE
EASY WAY

Is revising a shock to your system?

Get into it gradually by starting early
and plan your timetable so that in
week 1 you're doing 30–45 minutes a day.
In week 2, up it by 15–30 minutes a day.
From week 3, aim for 90 minutes
or more a day.

CUT

TO SIZE

How can you cut down revision?

Reduce it by working out what
you do know and what you don't
know. Concentrate on understanding
the 'don't know' topics.

STUDY

BUDDIES

Need to know you're not alone?

Then study with a friend. Agree to
study the same topic for a set time, say
20-25 minutes. After a 10-minute
break, revise by quizzing each other
for 10 minutes.

GREAT

MEMORY

How do you remember stuff?

Make revision notes exciting and colourful so they inspire your interest. Once your interest is ignited, your concentration soars and so will your retention of information.

TAKE

CONTROL

*Everyone keeps giving you revision advice.
What do you do?*

Listening won't hurt, but you have to
decide if the advice is helpful to you.
A successful revision plan is the one
that suits the way you learn and work.
You have to be in control!

HOW
TIME FLIES

Can't cope with studying for hours on end?

Studying for hours results in a bored
you and a tired brain, so don't do it.
Instead, think in minutes – 20–30
minutes focused studying, 10-minute
breaks. Measuring in minutes keeps
you on the ball.

BRAIN DRAIN
YOUR TEACHERS

Feel that school's a waste of precious revision time when exams are around the corner?

Not if you use those precious weeks getting your teachers to go over topics that are giving you grief.

THE BIG
EXAM SECRET

What are the examiners looking for?

Just three things – knowledge, understanding and skill. In other words – what you can remember, what you can explain and what you can do. Keep these in mind when setting revision priorities and assessing if you have mastered a topic.

ON YOUR
MARKS. . .

Getting started is the problem?

There's only one thing for it – give yourself a set time to start revising each day and stick to it. Equally crucial are short breaks and a set finishing time.

DON'T PUT
IT OFF

Need some tips for tackling those topics that don't come easy?

1. Make them a number 1 priority... NOW!
2. Break them into even smaller revision units.
3. Give yourself twice as long to revise them.
4. Test yourself after every revision session.
5. Get a study buddy to help and encourage you.

PLAN
AHEAD

What is an essay plan?

It is the first stage of a successful essay when you note down all the relevant points needed to fully answer the question. Number each point in the order they should appear in the essay.

READING

PLUS

How should you revise set texts?

Read a chapter in each revision
session and make notes under the
following types of headings: character,
theme, use of language, setting, plot
etc. When you've completed the text,
revise your notes to get an overview.

GET
EMOTIONAL

*Drama and poetry revision sending
you to sleep?*

Bring it to life by getting out of your
chair and reciting out loud soliloquies,
asides and verses on an imaginary
stage. Don't hold back on the emotion
and expression – the more you
put in, the greater the impression
on your memory.

ASK A
TEACHER

Can't master something and it's getting you down?

Stop struggling immediately – it's draining your energy and enthusiasm for revision to follow. Mark the problem and write yourself a note to ask the subject teacher for help the next day.

SPICE

IT UP

Why does revising have to be so boring?

It isn't if you vary your revision methods — reading, taking notes, testing, reciting out loud, working with a study buddy, listening to and watching audio and video tapes. Create colourful and memorable revision notes — posters, maps, flow charts and diagrams.

PRACTICE
MAKES
PERFECT

Is there any point doing practice essays?

Sure is! Practice essays really test your understanding and knowledge. Becoming confident and efficient at essay planning is very important, so when you haven't the time to write a full practice essay, take five minutes to write an essay plan.

EXAM READY

No sense of time?

Get used to working under time limits
by allocating 10, 20, 30 or 40 minutes
to revise a topic, do a test or write an
essay. This will make you familiar with
the time limits you'll allocate to
questions during exams.

EXPRESS
YOURSELF

Something worrying you?

Give yourself five minutes to jot down
in point form what's worrying you.
When it's straight in your mind, talk it
over with a teacher or someone in the
family. The problem may disappear or
you'll find a positive solution.

REVISION
PERFECT

Is your revision timetable working?

It is if you can answer 'yes' to
these questions:

1. Are you on top of your revision?
2. Are you scoring well when self-testing?
3. Are your revision notes shrinking?
4. Are you relaxed and feeling confident?

(Solutions for any 'no' answers follow.)

STAYING

ON TOP

Revising solidly, but feel overwhelmed?

Use a revision period to review how far you've come. Go through your subject/topic lists and give yourself a big tick or smiley face for every topic completed. Overwhelmed no more, but totally in control again.

QUIZ ME

Desperate to put your excellent revision to the test?

Re-do questions in workbooks and text books and re-take topic/module tests. Then ask teachers for copies of old term tests, buy past exam papers and check out the revision sites on the web. Do the tests with a time limit and no help.

AMAZING
SHRINKING
NOTES

*Revision notes threatening to take over
your room?*

When you start, your study notes will
be hefty, but as you revise each topic,
keep shrinking your notes until they
are just key words, charts and picture
prompts that will fit on an index card.

CRUISING

Revising is turning into a nightmare?

It could be that you're not giving
yourself quality time out from book
bashing. After each block of revision
have a 10-minute break and leave
plenty of time for rest and relaxation.

MARK YOUR
WORDS

Need some feedback?

Marking right or wrong questions is easy, but for extended written answers, ask a teacher to mark it. You and a study buddy could do the same question and then check each other's answers for organisation, correct facts and spelling, content and presentation.

SPELLING BEE

Do you want to up your marks by 5%?

Then brush up on your spelling so
that you don't lose marks. Ask an adult
to check your class and revision notes
for spelling mistakes and to write up a
list of correct spellings. Learn and quiz
yourself on 5-10 spellings each day.

LEARNING

CURVE

Is it any use revising the night before an exam?

Definitely! If you revise a topic that you have already studied, your recall the next day after a good night's sleep will be at its peak. However, material learned for the first time the night before an exam will not be effectively remembered the next day.

NO PROBLEMS

How do you learn really difficult stuff?

Break the material into small chunks —
sentence by sentence, if necessary.
Knuckle down to thoroughly
understanding one chunk and revising
it before going on to the next.

REINFORCE

Can't remember anything after reading it?

Reading isn't enough. Reinforce what
you're reading by reading it out loud,
writing notes in the margins and
highlighting important sections.
Follow up with notes in your own
words and self-testing.

NOTABLE NOTES

How can you make revision notes memorable?

Make them eye-catching by using lots of colour and keep them brief by using key words, abbreviations, diagrams, charts and illustrations.

KEYED UP?

What are keywords?

These are the words, dates and names – anything from one word to a dozen – that sum up a topic you have revised and understood. When you recall these words, they unlock the information stored in your brain.

INDEX IT

Can't find those important facts?

As you revise, write down must-know information, facts and difficult spellings or vocab on index cards. Store them in a box file under subject headings for rapid revision sessions. Once mastered, put that card to the back of the file.

FRESH

APPROACH

*Can't cope with lists of language
vocab and verbs?*

Break the list into groups of 5 to 8
words and meanings and revise one
group a day. Every four days, test
yourself by reciting and writing all the
words and meanings you have learned.
Any incorrect ones should be added
to the next group.

WACKY

WORDS

Do you need help remembering long lists?

Take the first letter of each word in the list and see if they make a word or short phrase. For example, the colours of a rainbow can be shortened to: ROY G BIV.

SWITCHED ON

Do audio and video revision tapes work?

If used in combination with active learning techniques like note-taking and self-testing, then tapes and videos are good revision aids.

MEMORY

JOGGER

Can't recall that last bit of information?

Just remember: who, what, when, where, why and how. Use these prompts to help you search your memory banks.

IN YOUR

FACE

Can't remember formulae?

Write the formula and what it's used for in enormous letters on a large piece of paper. Tape this on the fridge, behind the loo door, above your bed or next to your mirror.

. . . ONCE UPON
A TIME

Getting the chronology all wrong?

Turn the string of events into a totally off-the-wall, fairy tale-type story with a beginning, middle and end.

WAKEY, WAKEY

*Can you revise on the morning
of an exam?*

Non-stressful revision of something
already well-revised can help, but don't
change your routine to wake unusually
early. Give yourself plenty of time to
get ready – it takes 60 minutes after
waking for your brain to be working
at its peak level.

YOU MAY

COMMENCE

What should you do when the invigilator says 'You may commence'?

Give yourself a couple of minutes to read through the paper to allocate time for each question or section and to mark options you want to attempt.

TIME IT

*Don't know how long to spend
on each question?*

Be guided by the amount of marks
awarded for each question.
For example, it would be a waste
spending half the exam time on a
question that carries only 10% of
the marks.

DOWNLOAD

Worried that you'll forget something really important?

As soon as the exam starts, write down must-not-be-forgotten facts, dates, names and formulae somewhere on your paper. Once they're on the paper, you can stop panicking and turn your full attention to the exam.

SPOT CHECK

*How can you prevent answering the wrong
number or selection of questions?*

Carefully read all instructions and
mark the questions you are going to
do. As you start each question, double
check the instructions to make sure
you're doing the right thing. Better to
spend 5 seconds checking, than
5 minutes on the wrong question.

MAKE IT EASY

Why is presentation so important?

Easy-to-read handwriting, clear organisation and presentation, and clearly drawn and labelled diagrams make it easy for the examiner to spot every mark you have earned.

GO ALL

THE WAY

How detailed should answers be?

Assume that the examining marker knows nothing about the subject. This means your answer must contain enough clearly-expressed, relevant facts to bring him or her up to speed on the topic. Full answers score full marks.

READY AND
COUNTING

Need the fast lane for maths multiple choice?

Save time in maths multiple choice questions by mentally calculating what the last digit in the answer should be. For example: 334 x 412, the last digit will be 8 (4 x 2). Eliminate any answers that do not end in 8.

ONE STEP
AHEAD

How can you maximise time in comprehension or extract-type questions?

Read the questions before reading the text passage, and mark words or sentences that look likely to provide answers. Re-read the extract before putting pen to paper.

THE LAND OF
NEVER-EVER

What do you do if you don't know an answer?

Put a mark alongside the unanswered question and leave time to come back to it. You may remember the answer and get full marks, or gain some marks with an educated guess. Never-ever leave a question unattempted.

ON YOUR SIDE

Exams and examiners are out to get you?

Wrong! Exams are not trying to catch you out with sneaky questions and examiners are not looking for ways of taking away marks – they look for ways of giving you marks!

ONE FOR ONE

*What's better — long sentences
or short ones?*

Keep your sentences short by sticking
to the one fact per sentence rule.
This keeps essay-type answers punchy
and concise, and makes it easy for the
examiner to mark.

THIRD TIME
LUCKY

Why read and re-read essay questions before planning an answer?

From the first read, find out the topic and theme of the question. On the second, underline those words that tell you what form your answer should take. Plan your essay, then re-read the question to check you have completely answered the question.

QUALITY
COUNTS

In the exam, everyone but you is asking for extra paper?

Examiners are looking for
quality answers, not long ones –
so don't panic.

MIND-READING

Examining markers will know what you mean, won't they?

They are not mind-readers and they can't give marks for information that's not on the paper.

READ IT
IN THE PAPER

Totally lost for a word, idea or spelling?

If memory tricks yield nothing, then flick through the exam paper. You never know, you might just find the word you want or a link that nudges the information stored in your brain.

WORKING
IT OUT

Why should you show your working out?

If your final answer is wrong, the examiner can check the working out to see if you understood the question and had the knowledge and skill to do it. If it shows any of these, then you may gain a proportion of the marks.

BE PRECISE

Know the answer but miss out the crucial detail?

Think before you start writing!
Then, assess if your answer includes
the essential information or
precise term – often just one or
two words – that will earn full marks
for the question.

NO QUESTION
UNANSWERED

Haven't a clue about a multiple choice question?

Never leave a multiple choice question unanswered. Delete the off-the-wall answers, then choose the most likely answer from those remaining.

RUNNING OUT
OF TIME

Time allocation for each question has not worked out. What can you do?

To get marks for an essay-type question, plan your answer and write an introduction that shows you understand the question and can 'argue' your position. Then use point notes to show what facts you would have used in support. Finish with a brief, properly-worded conclusion.

USE THE
JARGON

How can you impress science paper examiners?

Using scientific terminology in a correct answer will earn full marks. Water, for example, doesn't disappear when boiled, it evaporates.

CHECK
OUT TIME

*How much time should you leave for
checking over your paper?*

It does depend on the format of the
paper, so you should ask the advice of
the subject teacher. A suggested time,
however, is five minutes.

Remember . . .

SUCCESS IS ALWAYS WITHIN
YOUR REACH!